Build a CULTURE of Excellence

A Blueprint for Transforming Communities,
Organizations, and Lives

JAMES THOMAS, ED.D.

Dedication

This book is dedicated to children who never had a voice or a loving listening ear—those whose stories were forgotten, whose suffering was ignored, and whose potential was never realized.

This book is a tribute to individuals who sought understanding but were met with silence, who wanted guidance but were left to confront life's challenges alone— your voice is important. Your efforts, tenacity, and goals deserve to be recognized, supported, and elevated.

This work should inspire communities, leaders, and mentors to listen compassionately, uplift consciously, and create circumstances in which every child feels heard, acknowledged, and valued. True brilliance is measured not by individual accomplishments, but by our ability to make sure no child goes forgotten, ignored, or mistreated.

Preface

During my career, I have seen the worst of human behavior and the profound influence of opportunity. With over twenty years of law enforcement experience, including my tenure as a Company Commander in the legendary Texas Rangers, I have led high-stakes investigations, hunted dangerous criminals, and carefully sought justice for victims. My time as a juvenile detention officer exposed the harsh realities that face adolescents caught up in the criminal cycle, which fueled my passion for intervention and prevention. I have seen how circumstances, environment, and insufficient supervision lead youth down dangerous paths. But I have also seen the powerful influence of mentorship, education, and opportunities for redemption. Our society must choose which one they will allow to flourish. Where the resources and human capital go determines the path we will travel.

In addition to carrying the badge, I am a lifelong learner who has dedicated myself to education. I have worked as an adjunct professor at several public universities, where I have had the privilege of mentoring future leaders. I still find it intriguing how the brain develops; how a young adult eventually pursues their lifetime dream of becoming a professional in their chosen profession. The responsibility of helping to facilitate that pursuit drives me even more today. My dissertation was on the influence of environmental factors affecting adolescent African American males. Studying this helped expand my understanding of the problems facing this important demographic in our communities and schools, emphasizing the important need for proactive solutions and intervention. This also reinforced for me the enduring power of education to shape a better future for this important segment of our society, and how I could help families and communities with shaping their minds toward a bright future, full of endless positivity and hope.

I founded Excellence Blueprint LLC because meaningful transformation starts with a solid foundation of beliefs, mentorship, and community support. I have dedicated my life to not only enforcing the law, but also to preventing young people from entering the criminal justice system. I must admit that the latter is more difficult—especially because of the influence of years of oversaturation of drugs, crime, and violence in our communities. Through practical experience, research, and community engagement, I have discovered that the most effective way to reduce crime is to address its root causes—substandard education, limited opportunities, fractured families, and a lack of positive role models.

This book exemplifies my long-standing goal of providing organizations, communities, and families with the tools they need to create environments in which everyone, especially young people, can thrive and lead amazing lives. I hope that the ideas in this book will spark meaningful thought, long-term change, promoting a future in which every child, despite circumstance, has the opportunity to thrive.

— Dr. James Thomas, Founder of Excellence Blueprint LLC

Table of Contents

A Journey to Culture:
The Foundation of Excellence

I was born in 1979 as the second child to Raymond and Thelma Thomas. My brother, Raymond, Jr., was born in 1977. I grew up in a small town on the eastern edge of Texas called Newton, which is the county seat of Newton County. The 2024 census estimated the population of Newton County to be slightly more than 11,903. We lived in the local projects for my first few years in life. I can still recall faint memories of running around chasing my brother on the streets right off of Martin Luther King Dr. It even snowed one day, and my mom took a photo of the family having fun in the snow. Snow was a rarity in that part of Texas.

Newton County is known for the vast timber industry that drives the local economy. My father worked in the industry, cutting wood and loading trucks. He would leave early in the morning for work, often before my mother woke us up for school. I recall waking up sometimes to tell him goodbye. I remember thinking my dad must be the strongest man in the world because of how he carried the chainsaw he used for work with one arm. I remember the days when I would run outside to offer to carry the chainsaw into the house. My dad would humorously let me carry it, laughing as he saw me struggling to carry it with two arms. I remember my dad always saying that the work was hard, but it was his responsibility to support the family, and that is what he had to do to make that happen.

We lived in various places in Newton County growing up, eventually ending up back on Martin Luther King Dr., commonly known as "The Hill" in Newton. Watching westerns was what my dad did when he was at home. On the weekends, if my brother and I came into the house from playing outside, most of the time, my dad was in the house watching westerns. It was a religion in our household. My mother would normally be cleaning or cooking when she wasn't sitting beside my dad watching the endless loop of westerns on television. My mom would sometimes watch westerns even when Dad was not at home. One day, I was in the house watching westerns with my mother when I saw the image of an actor playing a character who was a Texas Ranger. I was around the age of nine when I saw this actor on television. I told my mother that I wanted to be a Texas Ranger. From that moment forth, I committed my life to that goal, concentrating on being the best version of myself.

At ten, my brother and I began picking peas for our landlord, Mr. Gatson. He was a kind, soft-spoken older Black man who owned what seemed to be fields that went on forever. We would pick peas, watermelon, corn, and bail and stack hay for him during the summer. As I reflect, this taught me the value of hard work, being reliable, and how to provide a service and earn honest money. My mother would wake us up around 5:30 every morning in the summer. She would cook us breakfast and tell us to be careful when we left the house just before the break of day to walk just over a mile to Mr. Gatson's field to begin work. We would normally be done between noon and one o'clock. We would then walk home to grab a bite to eat. Soon after, we would find our friends and play basketball, football, or connect with some of our friends to create trails and shortcuts through the woods to get to and from our other friends' homes.

While growing up in Newton, Texas, my brother, friends, and I would play cops and robbers while we rode our bicycles up and down the winding hilly streets of our neighborhood on Martin Luther King Dr. I always wanted to be the officer. Humorously, despite my dogged determination to be the fastest and best officer, I didn't always catch the supposed bad guy because they were faster or had better bikes. When the game of good and bad was over, I learned to move beyond the game and realize that my brother and friends were never truly the bad guys; they were just participating in a game. This detachment worked for me. I never brought the playful activity of good and bad with me into the next day. Every day was a new day, and every opportunity was a new opportunity. These were lessons I carried with me through life.

In grade school, I achieved academic excellence, assisted my peers with homework, and dedicated myself to helping with the success of others. At Newton High School, where our mascot was an eagle, I provided tutoring for three years, held the position of vice president of the student council my junior year in high school, and took part in varsity athletics where I made the district first-team academic honors team and second-team athletic team for sports my senior year. These years instilled in me the importance of leadership, accountability, and teamwork. "Eagle Pride Never Dies" went beyond mere expression in my city; it embodied a cultural ethos. A culture that influenced me, tested me, and ingrained the significance of excellence in every part of life. This ethos embodies supporting each other regardless of race, class, or gender. Football was more than a sport for our small community; it seemed like a religion. It was a privilege to wear the purple and white and to call yourself an eagle athlete. Our coaches taught us life lessons, such as the person to your left and right were counting on you to do your part every play. Further, if you did not do your part, then the play would not work, and the end outcome would not be the excellence they envisioned when they called the play. Every play depended on you and the ability of every player to become one. The entire town seemed to close when the Friday night lights turned on. We could always count on the community being there, despite weather and location, to support their eagles on the field. The Eagles appeared in seven state championship games, winning five.

My passion for excellence pushed me to go to Lamar University in Beaumont, Texas. I became a resident assistant, helping incoming students transition into college life and living in dorms. I was employed at the financial aid office, which gave me an early elementary foundation of financial accountability and literacy. The wonderful professionals in that office taught me so much. In August 2001, I earned a Bachelor of Science degree in Criminal Justice, and shortly after that, I began training at the Texas Department of Public Safety's Recruit Training Academy. At the academy, I learned about the tragic and horrific events of September 11, 2001.

That moment solidified my sense of duty for the law enforcement profession. I wanted to protect and serve, not just as a law enforcement officer, but as a leader who could shape a better society.

Throughout my career, I held various positions, including with the Texas Highway Patrol as a Texas Highway Patrolman. While working an extra job at a Disciplinary Alternative Education Program campus, I encountered a 14-year-old African American male who was a leader amongst his peers. When I approached him, he responded with aggression, his demeanor obviously hardened by years of distrust and frustration. He clearly did not want to engage in conversation with me, and I was in no mood to deal with unnecessary confrontation. Later, I learned he was a Crip gang member who had been caught selling drugs on school property. I left that extra job a month later, never knowing what path he would take, but life has a way of teaching us lessons when we least expect them.

Then after receiving a promotion to the Texas Department of Public Safety's Criminal Investigations Division, I became a Special Deputy United States Marshal with the United States Marshals Service Gulf Coast Violent Offenders Task Force. Our goal was to locate and capture the most violent offenders in Harris County, home to Houston, the fourth-largest city in the United States. Most of the fugitives we pursued were young African American males, a concerning trend that reinforced my concern about the difficulties facing these individuals and the factors leading them down the path to violence.

One day, I received a new fugitive case file. As I stared intensely at the photo of the wanted fugitive, an uncomfortable sense of familiarity swept over me. The face staring back at me from the still image was all too familiar. It was the same young man I had encountered years before at the Disciplinary Alternative Education Program campus. He was no longer a disturbed adolescent grappling with the educational system and selling drugs; he had become a fugitive, wanted for capital murder. Capital murder is the most heinous offense in the Texas Penal Code.

My team and I apprehended him on the same day. When we arrived at his family member's home, I saw the pain in her eyes. His aunt wept, unable to comprehend that her nephew was following in the footsteps of his father and grandfather, both of whom had faced similar fates. I was in disbelief as well. I did not see the hardened fugitive that day; I saw the 14-year-old boy I had met years earlier. One question haunted me: What more could I have done then to prevent what was happening now?

The question became the driving force behind my doctoral research, which examined the influence of environmental factors affecting adolescent African American males. My studies revealed patterns, influences, and environmental failures that perpetuated cycles of crime and violence. But more significantly, I discovered solutions. Strategies grounded in engagement, mentorship, education, and leadership.

The CULTURE framework emerged from these experiences. The seven principles of Care, Understand, Listen, Teach, Utilize, Restore, and Enrich form the foundation of transformation for individuals, families, communities, businesses, schools, and government organizations. CULTURE extends beyond law enforcement and social services. It is a comprehensive method for leadership, development, and excellence applicable in every context.

I urge you to approach each chapter of this book by reflecting through the lens of your own experiences. Ask yourself: In what way does this relate to my organization? My school? My community? My life? How can I integrate these principles into my everyday routine to cultivate a culture of excellence?

The journey ahead is one of discovery, exploration, reflection, and action. CULTURE is for everyone, and collectively, we can create a future where excellence is an ideal and a reality. Let's begin.

Beginning with Why Mindset Matters

The mindset, not the strategy, is the first determinant of success. How a company's executives and employees think, feel, and act significantly impacts the company's culture. Persistent greatness is built on a growth mindset, which is characterized by welcoming challenges, appreciating effort, and viewing learning as an ongoing process. When people in an organization have faith in their own abilities to grow, create, and triumph, it helps the whole company.

Mindset drives behavior in a culture of excellence. Leaders who think in terms of abundance inspire confidence, encourage teamwork, and create an example for others to follow. Employees may speak their minds, act independently, and strive for excellence. With this positive mental framework of the world, people are more likely to persevere through challenging situations to create conditions in which they may flourish, rather than only survive.

A shift in perspective is the first step in developing a culture of excellence. Fostering a sense of purpose, building self-confidence, and reinforcing greatness being achievable through consistent growth are all parts of this process. An individual's strong mindset is an asset to the organization.

Without adopting the proper mindset, however, nothing meaningful can be accomplished. When carried out by people who lack conviction, dedication, or persistence, even the most ingenious plans fail. Negative attitudes that refuse to budge, such as a fixed worldview based on lack, fear, or both, stifle development. People avoid difficult situations, resist criticism, and run away from responsibility. This paralysis at the individual level of mindset creates inevitable stagnation at the entire organizational level.

A person's mindset affects their actions, feelings, and even brain waves, according to psychological research. Cognitive scientists have discovered a process called neuroplasticity that lets our brains change and adapt in response to new information and experiences. Our brains create new neural connections that strengthen resilience, openness, and action orientation when we maintain an attitude of growth and possibility in all that we do. A pessimistic outlook reduces creativity, heightens stress, and triggers fear responses, which lead to poor performance.

A shift in perspective can also generate creative new ideas. People with a fixed mindset fear failure and reject change, so they cling to old ways of doing things even when their industries are changing and the future is uncertain. But people who have a growth mindset and are resilient face change bravely and with an attitude of courage. They ask better questions, who purposefully challenge assumptions, and adapt with a bold purpose. The ability to quickly adjust course and keep moving forward even when faced with uncertainty is a key competitive advantage for businesses that cultivate this mental flexibility.

Mindset research also looks at how people make sense of their successes and failures. People with a fixed attitude usually take setbacks personally, viewing them as evidence they are inadequate. Those who adopt a growth mindset see setbacks as opportunities for learning and improvement. In high-performance settings, when failure is constant, reframing is important. Perseverance, recalibrating, and recommitting are mental rather than talent-based abilities.

An effective lens for cultivating an excellence-based mentality is the CULTURE framework. Psychological safety and emotional involvement are fostered when leaders demonstrate the ability to care. They learn to empathize and adjust their support networks to meet actual needs after they understand. They make better decisions by listening to others and gaining ideas. By sharing their knowledge and teaching, they help others grow and develop, which strengthens the organization's principles.

To utilize the strengths of team members is to believe in their potential and align talents with strategic priorities. When companies restore, they recognize when they have failed and work to improve in the face of hardship. When they say they want to enrich, they mean they want to improve the workplace for everyone.

The unsung hero of every success story is mindset. Our outlook on opportunities, our reactions to setbacks, and our social interactions are all influenced by this. Companies that make mindset a core value in their culture are usually more open, creative, and quick to adapt. They understand that knowledge may be imparted, but that faith in one's own capacity to grow, take charge, and make a difference must be nurtured.

This way of thinking is just as important outside of the office. Culture serves as a guiding principle in communities and workplaces, establishing norms for conduct and fostering connections between individuals. The attitude we bring to every interaction—whether it is with serving customers, engaging with stakeholders, or interacting with youth needing direction and guidance—determines whether we promote change or perpetuate the status quo. Instead of viewing CULTURE as a list, leaders should adopt a transformative mindset that sees every obstacle as a chance to grow, every person as competent, and every moment as meaningful.

Rather than being abstract, my grasp of mindset is grounded in my own experiences. My dream of being a Texas Ranger began when I was a little boy, and I never wavered from that determination. I did not wait for opportunity; I prepared for it. I studied, trained, sought mentors, and created a path where one did not clearly exist. That mindset—the belief that I could achieve what others considered unlikely—became my driving force. I followed that path with discipline and perseverance, and in time, I achieved my dream.

But I did not stop there.

I accomplished more than just joining the Texas Rangers; I also became the first company commander in the modern era of the Texas Rangers to have a doctorate. That differentiation did not emerge by accident but rather because of a deliberate mindset. The same mindset that lifted me from a young boy with a dream to a leader entrusted with one of the most respected law enforcement roles in the world. I know what having the right mindset can do. I can attest to its power. Success in life, in business, in school, or in law enforcement is a matter of mindset, and I have used that mindset to teach others.

At its core, excellence is more of a discipline than an endpoint. And that self-control starts with the firm belief that there is room for improvement at every level of society. A culture of excellence starts with a mindset of possibility, nurtured through intentional leadership and reinforced through the values embedded in CULTURE.

This is more than a framework—it is a movement. And it begins with you.

Introduction:
The Urgency for Change

Transitioning from a distinguished career in law enforcement to entrepreneurship was not merely a career change for me; it was definitely a calling. After years of pursuing violent offenders, investigating crimes against children, seeing the repercussions of broken families, and flawed culture within systems, I recognized the necessity to take further action. I tried to transition from enforcement and punishment to prevention and empowerment. My goal became clear: to engage the culture and create lasting change where it mattered most.

As a Texas Ranger and public safety leader, I saw the catastrophic impact of crime on individuals, families, and communities. I encountered youth who had been neglected by their surroundings, deprived of direction, support, and opportunity. Many were not intrinsically bad; they were simply products of circumstances that afforded them limited alternatives. They reflected what they saw and witnessed. So many children mimic the behavior they see often. Many gang members were recruited into the gang by someone they knew, often someone they trusted. I often asked myself, what would have happened if someone with compassion and empathy had stepped in sooner and shown concern? What if these young people were afforded access to valuable mentorships, education, and a society that recognized their potential and provided resources and guidance?

This insight ignited my passion for establishing Excellence Blueprint LLC. I recognized that genuine reform begins not with law enforcement, juvenile justice systems, or social work, but with cultural change. The values we impart within our homes, companies, schools, and communities influence the decisions individuals make. Using the CULTURE framework, I seek to help communities and businesses in establishing environments that empower youth to make informed decisions, inspire employees to lead with intention, and foster thriving families and communities through deliberate investment in excellence.

Alongside my considerable law enforcement experience and doctoral degree, I have a master's degree in behavioral science, enhancing my understanding of human behavior, motivation, and the environmental factors affecting decision-making. My academic background, coupled with real-world experience, has enabled me to bridge the gap between theory and practice in creating sustainable transformation and positive solutions. The CULTURE curriculum is the answer that many have been looking for. A solutions-driven process focused on establishing a culture of excellence that everyone can live and abide by in their personal and professional lives.

Throughout my career, I have received many awards and accolades for my commitment to excellence and service. In 2014, I was honored to earn the Outstanding Doctoral Student Award from Lamar University. I became the first contemporary Texas Ranger to obtain a doctorate degree, showing my dedication to both learning and public service. I had the distinct privilege of attending the 285th session of the Federal Bureau of Investigation National Academy, with 247 individuals from 48 states and 28 nations. In this esteemed school, I was appointed as the class spokesperson—an accolade awarded to a single graduate per session.

These accomplishments are not only individual milestones; they illustrate the power of perseverance, the transformational influence of education and leadership, and the unwavering quest to make meaningful change and public service.

Entrepreneurship has given me the opportunity to tackle difficult challenges proactively. I now focus on crisis prevention rather than crisis response. Rather than incarcerating, I focus on inspiration and deterrence. Rather than just responding to adversity, I try to cultivate resilience. My shift from law enforcement to business is grounded in my conviction that authentic leadership centers on impact, with the most significant influence occurring well before a crime is perpetrated.

This book is more than a mere guide; it serves as a blueprint for transformation. This is an appeal for leaders, families, educators, and community members to assume responsibility for the culture they create. To build a future free of crime, disengagement, and squandered potential, we must be deliberate in the ideals we champion. Excellence is not an accident; it is a cultivated ethos, and it starts with us.

Foundations of Excellence:
What it Takes to Transform Communities

Aculture of excellence is not a product of coincidence. It is deliberately constructed, with a strong foundation grounded in principles, vision, and steadfast commitment. Before examining the core principles of CULTURE, it is essential to comprehend the mindset and framework that help with lasting transformation. Excellence is not an isolated action but a consistent standard—a mindset, behavior, and leadership approach that enhances individuals, businesses, and communities.

Excellence originates from conviction. If we do not believe in the possibility of improvement, the existence of untapped potential in individuals, or the capacity for institutions to adapt, then significant change remains unattainable. Excellence is not synonymous with perfection; it encompasses development, resilience, and the endeavor to reach the best version of ourselves and others we help. Excellence is a constant endeavor, pursued in every moment, every action, every day. This belief system is the foundation of every endeavor to generate sustainable impact.

Establishing Core Values

Before cultivating a culture of excellence, a community or organization must define its core values. These values function as guiding principles that influence decisions, shape interactions, and set expectations. Core values such as empathy, integrity, trust, empowerment, and perseverance set a framework within which excellence can thrive. In their absence, initiatives to enhance systems and help individuals become fragmented and unsustainable.

For example, a youth organization focused on mitigating juvenile criminality must first adopt the principles of trust and empowerment before implementing intervention initiatives. Absent trust, youth will refrain from participation. Change will not last without empowerment. By articulating clear and concise values, organizations and communities guarantee that their initiatives are reactive and transformative. Organizations without clear and concise values often lack direction and leadership.

Core Values for Building a Culture of Excellence

Certain key values act as foundational pillars for establishing a culture of excellence. These values—empathy, integrity, trust, empowerment, and perseverance—are critical to my company and in developing individuals, organizations, and communities committed to long-term success. Each value is interconnected, supporting one another to form a strong culture that thrives on excellence, accountability, and purpose. We will go into detail about each of these essential core values below.

Empathy: The Heart of Human Connection

Empathy is the ability to comprehend and share the emotions of others. It is more than merely acknowledging feelings; it is actively trying to understand another person's viewpoint and experiences. Empathy is essential in a culture of excellence for creating diversity in thought and action, decreasing conflict, and strengthening connections.

Empathy is important in leadership and organizational growth. Leaders with empathy foster an environment in which employees feel valued and understood. This emotional intelligence improves communication, morale, and teamwork. In communities, empathy serves as the foundation for resolving societal issues such as juvenile criminality, educational gaps, and employment imbalances. Empathy may help businesses and individuals create trust, overcome gaps, and foster a sense of belonging.

Integrity: The Foundation of Ethical Leadership

Integrity is the commitment to doing what is right, even when no one is watching. It is honesty, consistency, and strong moral values. Integrity determines the credibility and reliability of individuals and organizations in every situation, including law enforcement, education, corporate leadership, and community involvement.

A culture of excellence cannot exist without integrity. When leaders maintain ethical standards, they create an example for those they lead. Integrity encourages transparency, accountability, and a sense of responsibility. Organizations that promote integrity see increased employee engagement, consumer trust, and long-term success. In community development, integrity guarantees that activities are motivated by real care rather than self-interest, resulting in meaningful and long-term impact.

Trust: The Cornerstone of Strong Relationships

Trust is the confidence in the reliability, truth, and ability of individuals and institutions. Without trust, collaboration suffers, growth is hampered, and dysfunction reigns supreme.

Trust must be carefully cultivated. In organizations, trust between leaders and employees leads to higher production, innovation, and job happiness. Employees who trust their leaders are more likely to take the initiative, raise problems, and contribute to the organization's mission. In law enforcement and community relations, trust influences whether individuals feel safe or excluded. Trust must be restored via attentive listening, consistency in behaviors, and a dedication to fairness and justice.

Transparency and accountability must not be compromised to preserve confidence. Leaders must communicate clearly, fulfill commitments, and be ready to admit and correct mistakes. Trust is fragile; once shattered, it is difficult to rebuild. Thus, cultivating a culture of excellence requires seeing trust as a valuable asset that must be fostered and protected.

Empowerment: Unlocking Potential and Driving Growth

Empowerment is equipping individuals with the tools, resources, and confidence they need to take control of their circumstances and contribute meaningfully to their environment. It is about providing opportunity, supporting autonomy, and promoting personal and professional development.

An organization that encourages empowerment understands that its most valuable asset is its people. Organizations foster an inventive, self-sufficient, and motivated staff by investing in training, mentorship, and leadership development programs. Empowerment contributes to higher engagement and job satisfaction because people feel their contributions are valued and their development is focused on.

Regarding community impact, empowerment is an effective technique for ending the cycle of poverty, crime, and alienation. When young people receive education, guidance, and chances, they are more likely to lead productive and meaningful lives. Empowerment is not about giving people authority; rather, it is about creating an environment in which they recognize their own ability to create change. This shift in thinking has a transformative effect on individuals and entire communities.

Perseverance: The Drive to Overcome Challenges

Perseverance is the steadfast determination to continue striving toward a goal despite obstacles, setbacks, and hardships. In the pursuit of excellence, challenges are inevitable. However, those that exemplify perseverance do not give up in the face of adversity; instead, they adapt, learn, and push forward.

The path to success is rarely straightforward. Organizations endure financial challenges, leadership changes, and market swings. Leaders must model perseverance by displaying resilience, optimism, and a problem-solving approach. A culture of excellence is based on the belief that failure is a chance for growth, learning, and creativity.

Perseverance is essential for self-improvement and long-term success in both personal and professional life. Many of history's most influential personalities struggled before reaching their peak. What distinguished them was their refusal to quit. Perseverance helps people acquire fortitude, patience, and an unrelenting devotion to their vision.

Bringing It All Together: A Unified Culture of Excellence

While each value —empathy, integrity, trust, empowerment, and perseverance—holds significance on its own, their actual strength rests in their cumulative impact. A culture of excellence is not developed by individual efforts; it demands a comprehensive commitment to incorporating these principles into daily interactions, choices, and leadership practices.

- Empathy makes sure relationships are built on genuine understanding and care.

- Integrity creates a standard of ethical behavior that fosters trust and credibility.

- Trust creates the foundation for collaboration, innovation, and sustainable progress.

- Empowerment unlocks potential, letting individuals and organizations thrive.

- Perseverance makes sure challenges are met with resilience and determination.

Together, these essential principles foster a culture in which excellence is more than an aspiration—it is a way of life. Organizations that focus on these principles will have greater cohesion, stronger leadership, and a long-term influence on the communities they serve. Individuals who absorb these values will approach life's challenges with purpose, confidence, and a desire to make a difference.

Culminating Thoughts

Building a culture of excellence is a constant process that needs devotion, thought, and deliberate action. These basic values serve as guiding principles for anyone looking to create an environment that promotes excellence. By incorporating empathy, honesty, trust, empowerment, and perseverance into our daily lives, we can work together to build a world where success is defined not just by achievement, but also by the beneficial impact we have on others.

The Power of Leadership and Vision

E ach step toward excellence requires leadership. The existence of ethical leadership in a family, school, government, or charitable organization is pivotal in establishing a culture of excellence. Leaders create the standard by exemplifying the behaviors they want to see in others. They guide with firm conviction, making challenging but necessary decisions to maintain standards of excellence.

Vision is equally significant. Absent a compelling vision, individuals lack both direction and the courage to persevere. A clear and succinct vision delineates what success looks like and serves as a catalyst for individuals and organizations to aspire to greater achievements, thus fostering the discipline required for realizing their goals. It serves as a reminder that every activity, despite its insignificance, contributes to a greater purpose.

Overcoming Barriers to Excellence

Excellence is fraught with challenges. Opposition to change, insufficient resources, and deeply ingrained negative cycles and attitudes might obstruct progress. Still, identifying these obstacles enables us to formulate solutions to overcome them. Marcus Aurelius reminds us that the obstacle is the way.

- Mindset Transformations: Many individuals, families, and organizations grapple with a fixed attitude, certain that conditions cannot change.

Transitioning to a growth mindset—where challenges are perceived as opportunities—fosters an environment conducive to learning, adaptation, and improvement.

- Resource Optimization: Although resources may be constrained, the strategic use of existing assets—such as partnerships, mentorship, and community engagement—can enhance impact.

- Consistency and Accountability: Excellence is not a one-time endeavor; it is an ongoing commitment. Ensuring accountability for individuals and organizations preserves elevated standards and fosters continuous improvement.

Establishing the Foundation

As we go into the ideas of CULTURE—Care, Understand, Listen, Teach, Utilize, Restore, and Enrich—be mindful that these principles are interdependent. They are interconnected parts of a framework that requires commitment, intentionality, and faith in the potential for transformation. By adopting a mentality of excellence and establishing a solid foundation, we equip ourselves and our communities for significant, enduring change.

CULTURE:
A Framework for Everyone

Excellence transcends any particular domain. It is not just the domain of government agencies, educational institutions, non-profit groups, or enterprises. Excellence is a shared responsibility, a collaborative effort requiring the active involvement of every entity and individual within society. The CULTURE framework—Care, Understand, Listen, Teach, Utilize, Restore, and Enrich—is intended to be universally applicable, setting a basis for transformation across many businesses and communities. Government agencies aiming to enhance public trust, corporations seeking to promote employee engagement, schools committed to student success, and non-profits trying to support marginalized communities can use the principles of CULTURE as a framework for sustainable and meaningful transformation.

Government: Creating Policies That Embody a Culture of Excellence

Local, state, and federal governments have a unique potential to integrate the CULTURE framework into policies, programs, and projects that affect millions of individuals. Public institutions establish societal expectations, and by embracing a culture of excellence, they can develop systems that emphasize effectiveness, accountability, and community welfare.

Policies grounded in *Care* make sure government initiatives target the needs of every community, especially the most vulnerable. A commitment to *Understanding* promotes data-driven decision-making that accurately represents the diverse realities of the constituents served. *Listening* to the voices in the community and determining their perspectives results in policies that are both effective and responsive. *Teaching*, both through workforce development programs and education initiatives, equips individuals with the information and skills necessary for success. Utilizing existing resources responsibly and more efficiently guarantees that taxpayer funds are maximized responsibly and with the heart of stewardship. *Restoring* communities affected by entrenched and persistent challenges shows a commitment to justice. Finally, *Enriching* lives through investment in cultural, educational, and recreational opportunities reinforces the social fabric of togetherness in society.

Cities that embrace CULTURE experience enhanced public trust, reduced crime rates, and increased civic engagement. The government is not merely an institution; it embodies the values it upholds. By cultivating a culture of excellence, policymakers and public officials establish an atmosphere favorable to the prosperity of all citizens.

For-Profit Entities: Propelling Business Success with Organizational Culture

Businesses of all sizes are increasingly acknowledging that excellence transcends mere revenue; it involves cultivating a legacy of influence. Employees are the essence of any enterprise, and companies that embrace CULTURE foster environments where innovation, productivity, and morale thrive.

When organizations embrace *Care*, they build environments that promote employee well-being and customer satisfaction. *Understanding* customer needs enables enterprises to adjust and innovate effectively. *Listening* to employees cultivates a workplace culture that encourages the open exchange of ideas and sustains high levels of engagement. *Teaching* through mentorship, training, and professional development enhances workforce competencies. *Utilizing* corporate resources to invest in community activities enhances public perception and brand loyalty. *Restoring* confidence following difficulties or challenges increases resilience. *Enriching* employees' professional and personal development produces loyalty and competence at all levels.

Many globally successful companies—those known for their influence and longevity—function according to these principles, whether spoken or intrinsically practiced. When businesses see CULTURE as an investment rather than a duty, they create success that extends beyond the bottom line.

Non-Profit Organizations: Enhancing Impact Through Culture

Non-profit organizations exist to support communities, often operating on the front lines. The efficacy of these organizations is linked to the culture they foster inside their teams and their outreach efforts.

A non-profit founded on the principles of CULTURE is more efficient, adaptable, and influential. *Care* guarantees that programs are crafted with compassion and respect for the communities they support. Understanding lets organizations tailor services according to actual demands instead of assumptions. *Listening* to stakeholders—whether donors, volunteers, or beneficiaries—results in more relevant strategies. *Teaching* through advocacy and education enhances the organization's mission. *Utilizing* existing partnerships and resources enhances efficiency and scalability. *Restoring* hope in communities that have endured adversity strengthens social connections and nurtures transformation. *Enriching* the lives of both the served and the servers builds a cycle of positive development that extends far beyond any individual undertaking.

Many non-profit organizations struggle because of limited resources; still, those that emphasize CULTURE garner more dedicated volunteers, long-term funding partners, and greater public trust. Excellence is determined not by the size of an organization but by its impact.

Schools: Cultivating Excellence in Learning

Education serves as the cornerstone on which future generations build their lives. Institutions that integrate the CULTURE framework into their mission and daily practices create learning environments where students feel valued, encouraged, and empowered to achieve.

Care is clear in classrooms where educators nurture both academic skills and emotional well-being. *Understanding* means acknowledging various learning styles, backgrounds, and the challenges students face. *Listening* to children, parents, and educators generates well-informed policies that address real needs. *Teaching*, which extends beyond just textbooks, encompasses mentorship, character development, and life skills. *Utilizing* new teaching methods and community partnerships expands the opportunity for student achievement well beyond the classroom. *Restoring* confidence in students who have faced academic or social difficulties promotes resilience. *Enriching* the educational environment by integrating arts, financial literacy, extracurricular activities, and leadership opportunities guarantees that students receive a comprehensive education upon graduation.

Schools that operate with a culture of excellence do more than provide education—they inspire. When students experience this environment, they internalize these ideas, influencing their future careers, families, and communities, perpetuating a positive cycle of development.

A Culture of Excellence is for Everyone

The strength and benefit of the CULTURE framework resides in its universality. Excellence transcends any singular industry or institution; it is a benchmark that all organizations, including governmental bodies, corporations, non-profits, and educational institutions, can aspire to reach. When CULTURE serves as the cornerstone for decisions, strategies, and interactions, transformation becomes inevitable.

By embracing a culture of excellence, we are not merely improving individual organizations; we are influencing the future of our communities and our world. Every entity, despite its goal or structure, can foster a society in which *Caring*, *Understanding*, *Listening*, *Teaching*, *Utilizing*, *Restoring*, and *Enriching* are ideals and lived realities. CULTURE is not exclusive to a certain industry; it is for everyone. By collectively embracing it, we unlock the complete potential of individuals, organizations, and entire communities.

Excellence is not just an outcome; it is a way of life. It starts with CULTURE.

Care:
Establishing a Foundation of Genuine Concern

Central to any successful business is a profound and unwavering dedication to care. Care is more than just a sentiment; it is an active and deliberate effort to uplift, help, and cultivate people within an organization or society. It entails acknowledging the humanity of every individual—be it a coworker, a student, or a youth in need—and deliberately choosing to contribute to their welfare and success.

A culture of excellence is established by leaders who focus on individuals above procedures, recognizing the real lives influenced by their actions rather than only focusing on numbers and policies. This requires the establishment of conditions in which individuals feel valued, acknowledged, and encouraged. Communities that focus on care establish mentorship programs, mental health resources, and efforts that foster personal and professional growth. They recognize that cultivating trust and a sense of belonging enhances engagement, motivation, and sustained achievement.

Caring is the foundation for strong relationships, effective leadership, and meaningful change. The overarching idea creates an environment in which people feel seen, heard, and valued. True care in an organization or community goes beyond surface-level gestures; it requires a persistent and conscious commitment to understanding the needs, difficulties, and goals of people. When leaders show genuine concern, it has a ripple effect: employees become more engaged, children become more motivated, and communities become more unified. This leadership does more than just address problems; it seeks solutions that empower people and create paths to success.

Care emerges in many ways, ranging from policies that promote employee well-being to efforts that help disadvantaged groups. A company that actually values its employees invests in professional development, work-life balance, and mental health services. A school that epitomizes care provides kids with mentorship, emotional support, and educational opportunities tailored to their talents. A caring community provides resources, safe spaces, and youth-empowering initiatives. In each situation, care is not an abstract concept; it is a palpable force that propels significant growth.

Care is an important tool for breaking the cycle of violence and delinquency while dealing with juvenile criminality. Many young people involved in the legal system have faced neglect, trauma, or a lack of positive role models. A care-oriented culture tries to address the underlying causes of these challenges rather than merely punishing the conduct. Communities can help young people succeed by providing mentorship, rehabilitation programs, and early intervention activities. Care-based efforts show to these people that their mistakes do not define them, but their ability to learn and change.

Care includes creating supportive workplaces. Organizations that incorporate care into their culture report higher employee happiness, retention, and productivity. Leaders who listen, advise, and advocate for their colleagues foster an environment in which innovation and cooperation thrive. Employees who feel valued are more inclined to go above and beyond, take pleasure in their work, and contribute to a healthy workplace culture. This same idea applies to educational institutions, law enforcement agencies, and any other organization that interacts with people daily.

Ultimately, care is the motivating force underlying transformative change. It fosters trust, improves connections, and creates situations in which people can thrive. Without care, norms and structures become meaningless and ineffectual. Focusing on care gives policies new life, transforms organizations, and enables individuals to fulfill their full potential. Care must be central to leadership and decision-making in all sectors, including business, education, and community service. Only then can we foster a genuine culture of excellence.

Example: A Mentorship Model That Transforms Lives

A compelling illustration of care in practice is a youth mentorship program that pairs at-risk adolescents with committed mentors. Research indicates that mentorship can markedly reduce juvenile delinquency and enhance scholastic achievement. Through my experience with youth in the legal system, I have seen how one compassionate adult may significantly change the course of a child's life. An effective mentorship program offers more than basic advice; it builds lasting relationships that instill confidence, resilience, and a sense of purpose in the mentee.

Supporting Data

According to research from the National Mentoring Partnership, at-risk children with mentors are 55% more likely to enroll in college, 78% more likely to engage in regular volunteer activities, and 130% more likely to assume leadership roles in their careers (MENTOR 2014). Communities with robust mentoring programs have reduced crime rates and enhanced academic achievement among kids. These figures underscore the undeniable truth—caring is not simply an act of compassion; it is a calculated decision.

Personal Insight

Throughout my career in law enforcement, I saw many young individuals whose lives took fatal turns due to the lack of care in their formative years. Numerous violent criminals I investigated were not intrinsically malevolent; they resulted from neglect, abandonment, and broken systems. It became clear that punishment alone would not be enough to disrupt the cycle of crime in troubled communities; rather, authentic caring and intervention before the acts of crime and violence are the key to drastically changing the negative spiral affecting some of our youth. This insight ignited my fervor to transition from law enforcement to effecting transformative change through my company, Excellence Blueprint LLC.

Genuine caring goes beyond verbal expression; it is manifested through deeds. In leadership, education, or juvenile justice reform, valuing care engenders constructive transformation that transforms individuals, organizations, and entire communities.

Understand:
Identifying the Root Causes of Juvenile Crime

U nderstanding is the cornerstone of real change. Leaders must not only see problems superficially but also strive to understand the underlying challenges, strengths, and demands of the individuals and communities they serve. This requires a dedication to continuous learning and a willingness to listen to others without incorporating biases.

In businesses committed to excellence, understanding breaks through the surface-level of awareness. It means examining data, identifying systemic problems, and tailoring solutions to target root causes instead of just symptoms. Leaders who emphasize understanding cultivate settings where informed choices yield significant results. They try to close knowledge gaps, making sure each method corresponds with the lived experiences of people affected.

Understanding is essential for fostering long-term change within businesses, communities, and institutions. Leaders must challenge their preconceptions and participate in meaningful discourse with those they serve. This participation is not passive; it requires intentionality, humility, and a never-ending search of knowledge. Leaders who foster understanding recognize that every situation has multiple levels, and that each person has a unique story that impacts their thoughts and behaviors. By adopting this approach, they position themselves to make informed decisions that address underlying issues rather than depending on quick remedies.

A culture built in understanding values diversity of ideas and experience. People in any organization come from a variety of backgrounds, have diverse skill sets, and face unique challenges to success. A leader who understands their team takes the time to learn about these distinctions and then applies that knowledge to create a more inclusive and supportive atmosphere. This could include developing regulations that accommodate diverse learning styles, eliminating systemic biases that stifle growth, or creating an environment in which employees feel comfortable expressing their concerns. When people feel understood, they become much more involved, driven, and dedicated to a common goal.

Understanding is especially important in youth crime prevention. Many young people who end up in the criminal justice system come from impoverished, traumatized, and unstable backgrounds. Rehabilitation initiatives will fail if the social and economic issues affecting their actions are not understood. Effective intervention programs stress knowledge by identifying the underlying reasons of delinquency and adapting support. Mentorship initiatives, positive male role models, mental health counseling, educational opportunities, and workforce development programs are all possible options. Leaders and politicians may reduce recidivism and give these individuals a meaningful opportunity at success by looking beyond the crime to the circumstances that led to it.

In education, understanding is the cornerstone for effective teaching and student engagement. A school system that lacks understanding treats all pupils as if they have the same needs, ignoring the fact that some require more assistance, different instructional techniques, or alternative resources. The finest teachers and administrators work to understand their students' strengths, weaknesses, and learning styles. They evaluate data not only to measure performance, but also to identify gaps and make changes that lead to more balanced learning environments. Schools that value understanding offer mentorship programs, provide resources for children in need, and develop curricula that reflect the diversity of their student group. When children feel understood, they are more likely to excel academically and attain the confidence required to thrive in their future efforts.

In business, understanding makes the difference between success and stagnation. Businesses that do not understand their employees and consumers risk losing trust, engagement, and long-term loyalty. Leaders that devote effort to understanding workforce dynamics understand what motivates their staff, what hurdles impede productivity, and what incentives encourage greatness. This deeper understanding enables them to develop policies that boost morale, increase retention, and promote creativity. Firms that understand their customers create products and services that actually suit their demands. They perform market research, assess trends, and actively solicit input to ensure their relevance and competitiveness.

A commitment to understanding builds better connections between law enforcement and the communities they serve. In many places, mistrust between police and citizens is caused by a lack of understanding and historical tensions. When officers take the time to connect with the community, listen to issues, and form relationships outside of crises, they bridge gaps and create a more successful environment for public safety initiatives. Programs that encourage officers to mentor adolescents, go to community activities, and receive cultural competence training reinforce the idea that law enforcement is more than just enforcing laws; it is also about serving and protecting people.

True understanding calls for an openness to change and a readiness to question established assumptions. It is not enough to presume that previous experiences or common solutions always apply to current problems. Leaders must constantly educate themselves, seek feedback from people who have firsthand experience, and change their plans. This continuous learning approach keeps policies, programs, and initiatives relevant and effective.

Understanding is more than a professional talent; it is a personal virtue that improves connections in all parts of life. Taking the time to understand people promotes empathy, cooperation, and mutual respect in families, friendships, the workplace, and society. It enables people to get past disagreements and find solutions that help everyone involved.

Awareness distinguishes reactive leadership from proactive, transformative leadership. It serves as the foundation for an excellent culture, making sure every decision, policy, and effort is based on actual knowledge and empathy. Without understanding, organizations risk stagnation, communities suffer divisiveness, and individuals feel ignored. However, with understanding, true development is possible. Leaders who focus on it drive success and inspire those around them to do the same, resulting in a long-term influence that goes far beyond their immediate reach.

Example: Community-Driven Solutions

A municipal consultancy initiative designed to mitigate juvenile delinquency exemplifies the application of understanding. Before enacting any policies, an organization can undertake comprehensive surveys and convene focus groups with youth, parents, educators, and law enforcement representatives. This method will probably uncover unforeseen obstacles, such as a deficiency of after-school activities and employment prospects, which contribute to delinquency. By gaining this deep insight, a city can formulate focused efforts that specifically tackle these deficiencies, resulting in a quantifiable reduction in youth crime rates.

Supporting Data

Research underscores the necessity of understanding community needs before making change. Multiple studies show that crime prevention strategies embedded in community engagement and input are more effective than traditional top-down approaches. Also, a report from

Afterschool.org found that after-school programs are a productive way to keep children away from delinquent behavior during the hours right after when school typically ends and parents are at work (Zavala 2023). This shows that genuine understanding and focused engagement can generate sustainable solutions.

Personal Insight

Throughout my career, I have seen the repercussions of decisions made without sincere understanding. As a law enforcement officer, I often encountered policies that, despite being well-intentioned, did not effectively handle the practical realities. During my tenure with the U.S. Marshals Service Gulf Coast Violent Offenders and Fugitive Task Force, I saw how young men—predominantly African American males—became ensnared in cycles of criminality because of environmental circumstances well beyond their ability to control, and often were reinforced by years of financial and educational neglect in the communities in which they live. This insight pushed me to explore the influence of environmental factors affecting at-risk adolescents, hence informing my doctoral study and my mission with Excellence Blueprint LLC.

Understanding is more than just acquiring knowledge; it is about applying the knowledge reached to make real change, lasting change. When leaders dedicate themselves to understanding the individuals they serve, they pave the way for a brighter future built on informed, compassionate, and effective solutions.

Listen:
Giving Youth a Voice in Their Own Future

Aculture of excellence is established on a foundation of trust, which begins with listening. Active listening is not just simply hearing words; it entails a deliberate effort to comprehend, sympathize, and respond with intention. When organizations genuinely commit to listening, they create an environment in which individuals feel acknowledged, valued, and supported. This promotes transparent communication and is an essential initial step in effectively tackling challenges. Harrison & Gorman (2017) assert that when young people, especially those from marginalized backgrounds, feel heard, they are more likely to engage positively with support systems and make constructive life choices.

Listening encompasses verbal communication and the observation of body language, the understanding of unexpressed emotions, and creating an environment that lets individuals articulate their thoughts freely. By emphasizing listening, organizations and communities can more effectively evaluate the underlying causes of challenges, such as trauma, lack of resources, deficiencies, or barriers, and execute impactful solutions customized for the people they help. Brown (2018) emphasizes that effective listening cultivates relationships and strengthens emotional connections, helping with conflict resolution and promoting resilience.

A culture of excellence thrives when people feel heard, understood, and respected. Active listening provides a trusting environment in which people are more likely to discuss their concerns, voice their views, and collaborate on solutions. Leaders who focus on listening empower their teams, students, and community members by showing their voices are valued. When people feel heard, they become more committed to common goals, which fosters teamwork and shared accountability. Organizations that do not listen risk alienating their employees, pupils, or clients, resulting in apathy, resentment, and inefficiency.

True listening involves more than just waiting for one's chance to speak. It takes a deliberate effort to comprehend what is being said, both audibly and nonverbally. This entails acknowledging emotions, interpreting tone, and recognizing unstated conflicts that may affect conduct. In professional contexts, leaders who actively listen to their staff can discover workplace difficulties, uncover inefficiencies, and develop solutions that boost morale and productivity. An executive who listens to employee feedback on burnout, for example, may introduce wellness initiatives to improve work-life balance and job satisfaction. This proactive approach not only increases employee loyalty but it also fosters a culture in which people feel valued and inspired to put forth their best efforts.

In education, listening is essential for student achievement. Educators who carefully listen to their students can have a greater understanding of learning challenges, mental health issues, and external constraints on academic achievement.

When teachers create a classroom environment that promotes open communication, students feel more at ease expressing their needs, seeking help, and taking part in their education. Schools that employ student advisory boards, peer mentorship programs, and regular feedback sessions show a willingness to listen, which leads to higher academic performance and student well-being.

Listening is an important technique in juvenile justice and crime prevention efforts because it addresses the underlying reasons of misbehavior. Many young people involved in the court system have faced neglect, abuse, or systematic disadvantages. When law enforcement officers, counselors, and community leaders take the time to listen to these people, they can gain a deeper understanding of the conditions that led to criminal activity and create rehabilitative programs that provide actual solutions. For example, a study by Walton et al. (2021) introduced a relationship-orienting intervention where students reentering school from juvenile detention wrote letters to educators expressing their aspirations and challenges. This approach reduced recidivism from 69% to 29% in the following semester. The study suggests that fostering positive relationships between students and educators can improve outcomes for at-risk youth.

Listening is also essential for community growth. When local governments and groups actively ask for feedback from locals, they can change projects to meet specific community needs. Town hall gatherings, community forums, and participatory decision-making processes enable people to express their problems and propose solutions. This method promotes civic engagement and makes sure policies and programs are established with people's needs in mind. For example, a city experiencing increased crime rates may discover that locals blame the problem on a lack of youth programs, economic prospects, or mental health options. Listening to these insights lets local authorities better allocate resources, investing in initiatives that directly address the root causes rather than depending exclusively on punitive measures.

Listening is also important for promoting participation in the workplace. Many businesses and institutions face a workforce that does not feel engaged, thusly alienating part of the employees from decision-making about important metrics for the company. When leaders listen to different employees' experiences, they may develop rules that encourage engagement. Listening-centered initiatives such as employee resource groups and anonymous feedback platforms help to create a more engaged workplace. According to a study by ILR Assistant Professors John McCarthy and JR Keller, "Managers who are open to employee input are more likely to attract workers from other units in their organizations" (Cornell Chronicle, 2021).

Listening promotes emotional resiliency. In times of crisis, people who feel supported by active listening are more likely to overcome hardship. Mental health practitioners emphasize that being heard can be just as therapeutic as receiving advice. When companies and communities build support networks in which people can openly express their challenges without fear of being judged, they foster well-being and growth.

Finally, listening is an essential part of effective leadership, societal transformation, and corporate success. It is not a passive behavior, but a conscious effort to comprehend and respond to the needs of others. When firms focus on listening, they create environments in which people feel valued, engaged, and empowered. Whether in business, education, law enforcement, or community development, excellent listening turns obstacles into opportunities and enhances relationships at all levels of society. A culture of greatness can only be achieved when people believe that their opinions are heard, valued, and considered.

Example: Community Listening Circles

A city grappling with escalating juvenile crime collaborated with local organizations to conduct Community Listening Circles, wherein law enforcement officials, educators, and community leaders took part in candid discussions with at-risk adolescents. Rather than lecturing, they engaged in active listening, letting young people express their frustrations, anxieties, and ideas. A young man, who had mistrusted authority figures, found that these discussions made him feel seen for the first time. Supported by attentive mentors, he engaged in vocational training and turned away from his illegal lifestyle over time. His narrative exemplifies the profound influence of attentive listening.

Supporting Data

Research highlights the significant influence of listening on youth development and achievement. Research conducted by the Harvard Graduate School of Education revealed that when students perceive themselves as acknowledged and encouraged, their school involvement rises by 40%, resulting in a notable decrease in dropout rates. When adolescents perceive the significance of their voices, they are more inclined to remain engaged in their education and future prospects. Professionals must also recognize that developing effective communication with the adolescents with whom they work requires effort. It may take several sessions of nonjudgmental listening to establish the trust needed for a particular adolescent to share with an adult what they are thinking and feeling. It may even take longer before an adolescent feels comfortable asking an adult for help with an important decision (American Psychological Association, 2002). When youth feel appreciated and understood, they develop a heightened sense of purpose and are more inclined to make constructive life decisions.

Personal Insight

During my time in law enforcement, I encountered many adolescents who felt silenced by their circumstances. Many minors involved in the juvenile justice system have not been given a platform to express themselves in a way that leads to productive solutions. During instances when I took the time to listen, without bias or disruption, I saw significant breakthroughs. When adolescents perceive that their voices are heard, they show increased receptiveness to advice, are more willing to trust, and are increasingly motivated to change. Listening is not a passive endeavor; it is an active investment in transformation.

Listening is an essential tool to curate an environment of productive change. When we listen with empathy and intentionality, we construct pathways to trust, growth, and unbelievable change.

Teach:
Equipping Youth with Knowledge, Skills, and Purpose

Education is a powerful tool to create change. Taking the time to teach others what you know is pivotal. A culture of excellence focuses on giving individuals the knowledge, skills, and mindset necessary for succeeding. When corporations engage in teaching others leadership, life skills, and critical thinking, they empower individuals to break cycles of adversity and unlock their full potential.

Authentic teaching goes beyond the classroom. It involves mentorship, coaching, and practical application of skills. Organizations dedicated to excellence guarantee that teaching is an ongoing endeavor, providing professional development opportunities for staff and engaging educational initiatives for youngsters. These initiatives result in a more competent, capable, self-sufficient community.

Teaching is a critical part of cultivating an excellent mindset. It is sharing knowledge, honing abilities, and empowering individuals to take responsibility for their destinies. When leaders, educators, and organizations commit to teaching, they foster an environment in which learning is ongoing and possibilities abound. Education has a far-reaching impact that helps families, workplaces, and entire communities. A knowledgeable and talented populace is better prepared to face difficulties, make informed decisions, and contribute to society's progress.

Organizations that value teaching understand that their success is inextricably related to the growth of their employees. Businesses that invest in leadership training, skill development, and career advancement programs create a more productive and loyal workforce. Employees who receive continual education are more likely to innovate, adapt to change, and assume leadership positions. Companies that fail to give learning opportunities often face stagnation, high turnover rates, and low morale. A workplace that values continual learning encourages creativity, problem-solving, and teamwork, which are necessary for long-term success.

Teaching is also essential in tackling social issues, notably in youth crime prevention. Many young people take part in delinquent behavior because they lack supervision. When communities engage in mentorship programs, life skills training, and vocational education, they give young people alternatives that keep them out of trouble. Teaching these people important skills like financial literacy, emotional control, conflict resolution, and decision-making gives them the tools they need to live stable, prosperous lives, free of crime and violence. Education is a proactive approach to crime, providing empowerment and opportunity instead of punishment and isolation.

Teaching is important for leadership growth. Effective leaders are effective decision-makers and educators who impart their knowledge and experiences to those they lead. A leader who values teaching ensures that their team has the knowledge and confidence required to complete essential tasks successfully. This fosters a culture in which people are encouraged to learn, take initiative, and develop their leadership skills. Strong leaders recognize that their success is judged by the development and accomplishments of people around them. They build a teaching culture, resulting in businesses that are strong, flexible, and focused on continual improvement.

Education is also a valuable instrument for promoting growth within the community. Many societal inequities result from a lack of access to high-quality education and resources. When organizations and institutions make education available to everyone, they level the playing field and provide opportunities for people to succeed. Scholarships, free training programs, and mentorship projects that bridge the gap between knowledge and opportunity are great examples of this. Teaching must be wide-ranging, understanding that each individual has unique learning needs and adjusting educational approaches.

Authentic teaching also emphasizes experiential learning, which lets students apply what they have learned in real-world settings. People learn best when they can apply theory to practice, whether through internships, apprenticeships, or hands-on training programs. Organizations that incorporate experiential learning into their development programs make sure education is academic, practical and effective. This method develops a skilled, self-sufficient workforce and community capable of confidently facing obstacles and grabbing opportunities.

A trustworthy culture of excellence views teaching as a continuous process rather than a one-time event. To remain relevant in an ever-changing environment, knowledge and skills must be updated regularly. Organizations that develop a commitment to learning in response to changing landscapes maintain their competitiveness and innovation. They recognize that education is an investment not only in individuals but also in the organization's long-term viability and success.

Ultimately, teaching is a form of empowerment. It is how people develop the ability to improve their own lives and contribute to bettering society. A culture that promotes education makes sure no one is left behind by sharing knowledge, developing skills, and creating opportunities. Whether in businesses, schools, or communities, a dedication to teaching transforms lives, strengthens organizations, and creates a future in which excellence is a goal and a reality.

Example: Entrepreneurship for At-Risk Youth

A neighborhood organization can start an entrepreneurial course aimed at at-risk youth, focusing on financial literacy, business planning, and leadership skills. For example, a young man, once engaged in minor criminal activities, used the skills acquired to establish a small business specializing in personalized t-shirt sales. In one year, that individual generated enough revenue to support himself, showing teaching valuable skills and providing opportunity can serve as a pivotal turning point.

Supporting Data

Statistics illustrate the transforming impact of teaching. The National Dropout Prevention Center (n.d.) highlights information from the Alliance for Excellent Education's 2003 report that states structured after-school programs provide economic benefits, with an investment of $10,038 per participant yielding benefits of $89,000 and $129,000. This clearly underscores the quantifiable effectiveness of such programs in fostering positive youth development and reducing the likelihood of criminality. Likewise, research conducted by the U.S. Department of Labor (2019) has invested over $200 million in Reentry Employment Opportunities (REO) programs, equipping justice-involved individuals with valuable skills to improve employment prospects and lower reoffending rates. Also, the Mackinac Center for Public Policy (2023) found that prison education programs, including vocational training, reduce recidivism by 14.8%, increase employment likelihood by 6.9%, and raise quarterly wages by an average of $131. These statistics underscore the undeniable link between teaching, education, and favorable life outcomes.

Personal Insight

Personal and professional experiences have let me witness firsthand the power of teaching. As a Texas Ranger, I encountered young offenders whose paths could have been drastically different had they been given the right guidance and knowledge earlier in life. As an educator and adjunct professor, I have had the privilege of shaping minds and seeing the direct impact that teaching has on individuals. When we invest in teaching, we are investing in building safer, stronger, and more resilient communities.

Utilize:
Unlocking Potential and Mobilizing
Resources for Maximum Impact

A culture of excellence recognizes the importance of utilizing all available resources and opportunities to drive change. Organizations must identify and leverage their internal strengths, strategic partnerships, and technical resources to optimize their reach and effectiveness. Properly using resources makes sure individuals, especially adolescents, have access to the tools they need to succeed.

Successful organizations assess the abilities and potential within their teams and communities, matching them with activities that yield measurable results. They also forge partnerships with businesses, educational institutions, and nonprofit entities to increase opportunities for growth and development.

A culture of excellence requires effective resource utilization. Organizations that effectively assign their assets—whether financial, human, technological, or informational—are better positioned to effect substantial and long-term change. When organizations grasp the full spectrum of their resources and match them with their mission, they increase their impact and efficiency. Neglecting to use resources effectively can result in wasted potential, inefficiency, and missed possibilities for growth and innovation.

One of the first steps in resource utilization is to undertake a thorough assessment of internal strengths. Every organization, whether a corporation, nonprofit, or government institution, has distinct assets that can be used for success. This encompasses staff skills and knowledge, institutional knowledge, and corporate culture. Identifying these skills enables leaders to efficiently assign responsibilities, making sure each team member is positioned in a position that maximizes their abilities. For example, a school district seeking to promote student engagement may use experienced educators to mentor rookie teachers, making sure best practices are passed down and efficiently applied.

Strategic alliances are also important for resource use. No organization operates in isolation, and collaboration often results in increased efficiency and innovation. Organizations can broaden their reach and share their resources by developing alliances with businesses, educational institutions, and non-profits. For example, a corporation devoted to workforce development may collaborate with a local university to offer internship programs that give students real-world experience while also building a skilled staff pipeline for the company. Similarly, law enforcement agencies aiming to reduce juvenile crime can partner with community organizations to offer at-risk adolescents mentorship, job training, and educational resources as alternatives to criminal conduct. Also, law enforcement agencies needing qualified and willing candidates can create a pathway to attract and develop future recruits.

Technology is another strong resource that, if used properly, may boost productivity, improve communication, and enhance outcomes. Organizations that use digital tools, data analytics, and automation improve efficiency and make better decisions. Schools, for example, can use online learning platforms to give students tailored educational experiences, making sure each student has the help they require to succeed. Businesses can use customer relationship management (CRM) systems to track customer interactions and improve service delivery. Community organizations can use social media and digital outreach to interact with marginalized populations and provide useful information about services.

In addition to leveraging internal resources and technology, firms must seek external funding and financial resources. Grants, sponsorships, and philanthropic gifts can help an organization undertake programs and activities that generate change. Nonprofit organizations, for example, often rely on grant financing to extend their services, but enterprises may seek investment or government incentives to spur expansion and innovation. Organizations that seek financing possibilities and manage their financial resources are better positioned to achieve long-term success.

Human capital is a highly important but underutilized resource in many companies. Employees, volunteers, and community members each provide distinct perspectives, talents, and experiences that can help an organization succeed. When leaders focus on employee growth and engagement, they create a motivated workforce dedicated to the organization's mission and goals. This can be done through professional development programs, leadership training, and opportunities for team members to take on more important duties. Encouraging people to share ideas and take initiative develops an environment of innovation and continual progress, and ensures the network of trained and willing professionals continues for generations.

Using resources is also important in solving social issues, especially in adolescent crime prevention. Many towns already have resources in place, such as after-school programs, recreational facilities, and other networks, which could be effective deterrents to delinquent behavior among youth. However, these resources are often underfunded, underutilized, or distant from the communities that require them the most. By identifying and promoting these assets, communities may develop comprehensive support systems that give young people good ways to spend their time and energy. "Studies have shown that the most essential requisite for programs to reduce delinquency is that they provide structured, supervised activities to youth." (Kurtz, 2015).

Sustainability is another important issue while utilizing resources. A culture of excellence prioritizes not only short-term profits, but also guarantees that resources are set aside in a way that promotes lasting success. This includes putting in place processes for tracking and measuring outcomes, making data-driven decisions, and constantly evaluating the effectiveness of resource allocation. Organizations that take a strategic approach to sustainability achieve lasting change rather than momentary gains.

Successful resource utilization calls for an adaptable and continuous-learning mindset. The demands of communities, businesses, and individuals are continually changing, and organizations must be ready to reassess and shift resources as needed. Flexibility enables leaders to adjust to developing issues and seize new opportunities. For example, during the COVID-19 pandemic, many businesses and educational institutions were forced to transition to remote operations quickly. People who successfully used digital resources and adjusted to changing conditions continued serving their audiences effectively with fewer interruptions in operations.

Lastly, the proper use of resources is what makes vision a reality. An organization can have a strong mission, dedicated workers, and ambitious goals, but without a systematic approach to resource allocation, success is limited. Leaders who identify and use their teams' talents, form solid alliances, embrace technology, gain financial backing, and promote sustainability provide the groundwork for long-term success. A culture of excellence is more than just having resources; it is also about knowing how to apply them effectively to achieve significant and lasting transformation.

Example: Workforce Development Through Community Partnerships

A city program partnered with local businesses and universities to provide job training and internship opportunities for at-risk youth. This initiative gave participants practical experience across several industries, including technology and skilled trades. A young man, previously uncertain about his future, received an apprenticeship in vehicle repair and, within two years, became a certified mechanic with stable employment.

Supporting Data

Research shows that mentorship and workforce development programs reduce youth unemployment rates by 25% and significantly decrease the likelihood of involvement in criminal activity (National Youth Employment Coalition, 2020). Also, a report from the Brookings Institution highlights that federal investments in sector-based training can enhance economic mobility, with communities investing in skill-based programs seeing an 18% increase in long-term upward mobility for participants (Liu & Parilla, 2022).

Personal Insight

After a long career in law enforcement, I have seen many adolescents fall into a life of crime due to a lack of opportunities. So many had promising potential but lacked guidance and access to resources that could have launched them down a different path. Seeing this disparity firsthand motivated me to concentrate on developing solutions that empower adolescents and preempt crime before its inception. As a university professor and former law enforcement recruiter, I know what it looks like to work with individuals who excelled after being linked to the right opportunities. The difference between success and failure often lies in how well people use the resources available to them.

A culture of excellence is founded on strategic resource allocation. By effectively utilizing every resource and tool, we can forge pathways to success and guarantee a more promising future for individuals and communities.

Restore:
Healing Harm and Rebuilding Trust

A culture of excellence encompasses intervention and restoration. Genuine restoration is much more than addressing mistakes; it emphasizes healing, rebuilding, and the establishment of opportunities for permanent change. When individuals, particularly youth, encounter trauma, failure, or difficulty, they often feel a disconnection from their community and their potential. By cultivating a culture that emphasizes restoration, we provide second chances and avenues for redemption, development, and renewed purpose.

Restoration is repairing what has been broken, be it trust, confidence, or a sense of belonging. Many young people caught in the negative cycle of crime or hardship perceive themselves as defined by their past, convinced that their mistakes dictate their destiny. Research indicates that rehabilitation initiatives focusing on restoration yield superior long-term results. Programs that integrate mentorship, community reintegration, and emotional support help people to reconstruct their lives and productively contribute to society. Zehr (2015) asserts that restorative justice methods emphasizing healing rather than vengeance promote accountability and offer essential support for genuine transformation. Restoring an individual's dignity and self-worth empowers them to envision a future beyond their current circumstances.

Restoration is a key part of every flourishing community. A restoration-focused culture tries to actively fix broken paths and generate new opportunities for growth, rather than simply acknowledging previous faults. This approach is especially important when working with at-risk children, who often feel alienated because of previous mistakes, negative childhood experiences, or societal impediments. When these individuals are paired with established support systems that focus on restoration over retribution, they are more likely to reintegrate into their communities. Restoration tries to elevate someone to a level of renewed confidence, purpose, and belonging, rather than returning them to their pre-disaster status.

Restoration is critical for repairing trust in families, schools, and workplaces. Trust is sometimes one of the first casualties when people make mistakes or endure adversity. Youth who have experienced neglect, abandonment, or trauma may develop deep-seated sentiments of distrust, which can lead to disengagement from school, reluctance to seek treatment, or separation from positive influences. Restoring trust requires patience, consistency, and a sincere desire to mend relationships.

Some research suggest that restorative approaches lead to significant changes in student conduct, engagement, and academic success. "Restorative practices are designed to build a strong sense of community in schools, to teach interpersonal skills, to repair harm when conflict occurs, and to proactively meet students' needs—including those that result from trauma in or outside of school—so misbehavior is less common" (Learning Policy Institute, n.d.). Instead of expelling or suspending students for disciplinary infractions, many schools now use restorative circles, peer mediation, and conflict resolution tactics to encourage kids to take responsibility while still taking part in their education. These strategies not only prevent repeat offenses, but they also help children learn important life skills like communication, emotional regulation, and problem solving.

In the workplace, companies that promote a culture of restoration rather than blame create situations in which individuals feel comfortable learning from their mistakes. This technique improves team bonding and fosters innovation. Employees who know they will be supported in their development rather than punished for mistakes are more likely to take the initiative, provide fresh ideas, and form important professional relationships.

Restoration spans from people to entire communities. Many neighborhoods affected by high crime rates and economic hardship experience a sense of pessimism and alienation. Community-based restoration projects aim to rehabilitate these communities by addressing disparities, helping with youth engagement, and promoting collective healing.

Mentorship programs, for example, connect young people to well-known professionals in their areas, providing important assistance and inspiration. These programs empower adolescents with role models who show that success is possible despite hurdles. Similarly, organizations that specialize on workforce development help formerly incarcerated people reintegrate into society by providing vocational training, job placement services, and financial literacy education. These initiatives produce a ripple effect by giving individuals the skills and resources they require to succeed, thus strengthening families and revitalizing entire communities.

Another critical part of community restoration is the promotion of mental health and wellness. Many people who face adversity or take part in criminal behavior do so in response to unresolved trauma, a lack of emotional support, or unfulfilled psychological needs. Community centers, faith-based organizations, and mental health specialists all play an important role in providing accessible counseling, support groups, and wellness initiatives to help people process their experiences and build healthy coping strategies. When mental health is focused on, people can face challenges better, create resilience, and contribute productively to society.

Education is also a key part of the restoration process. Knowledge is a transforming tool that enables people to overcome their circumstances and pursue significant opportunities. Educational institutions that adopt restorative techniques reduce dropout rates and foster a culture of personal responsibility and continual learning.

Programs that provide second-chance education, such as GED completion courses, vocational training, and college reentry efforts, allow individuals to re-engage with their education despite earlier obstacles. These programs are especially important for young people who have left school due to disciplinary concerns, financial hardship, or personal difficulties. Institutions play a critical role in restoring hope and creating new opportunities by reducing barriers to education and offering specialized support. Teaching life skills such as financial literacy, conflict resolution, and emotional intelligence makes sure students are academically prepared and ready to face real-world issues. Schools that incorporate these lessons into their curricula help adolescents develop the self-esteem and resilience required for success.

Maybe one of the most important parts of restoration is the rediscovery of purpose and identity. Many people who have endured substantial challenges suffer with emotions of unworthiness or aimlessness. When organizations, mentors, and communities invest in restoring a sense of purpose, they enable people to see a future beyond their current circumstances.

Individuals can positively reframe their identities through programs that promote entrepreneurship, creative expression, and leadership development. Arts-based therapy projects, such as those that let young people express themselves via music, painting, or storytelling, offer therapeutic outlets for trauma processing. Likewise, leadership programs that teach young people how to advocate for their communities foster a sense of agency and responsibility.

Faith-based and personal development organizations play an important role in identity restoration. Many people who feel lost or alienated find comfort in spiritual guidance, personal mentorship, and structured self-improvement programs.

These pathways help individuals in reconnecting with their values, setting meaningful goals, and developing supportive networks that promote their progress. A culture of excellence tries to restore individuals, relationships, and communities to their full potential rather than simply correcting flaws. True restoration requires a strong commitment to healing, rebuilding trust, and generating chances for transformation. Organizations may improve lives and create settings in which people feel valued and supported by focusing on relationship repair, investing in community-based projects, and using education as a vehicle for empowerment. Restoration is more than just giving people second opportunities; it is about reimagining what is possible for individuals who have overcome adversity.

When societies choose restoration as a guiding principle, they break the cycle of failure and disenfranchisement, replacing it with paths to hope, progress, and excellence. In doing so, they promote not only individual success but also social prosperity, making sure no one is forever defined by their past and that everyone has the opportunity to contribute to a healthy future.

Example: The Youth Reintegration Project

A community grappling with elevated juvenile recidivism rates instituted the Youth Reintegration Project, a program aimed at helping young offenders in effectively reintegrating into their communities. The program focused on connecting participants with mentors, vocational training, and counseling services, rather than concentrating exclusively on past offenses, to help with their reintegration into society. A young guy, who had experienced the system occasionally since the age of 14, was allowed to collaborate with a mentor who recognized his ability. With consistent coaching and an organized support system, he completed his schooling, obtained stable employment, and became a mentor. His conversion exemplifies the efficacy of rehabilitation—not just for the person, but for the entire community.

Supporting Data

Research from the National Institute of Justice says young offenders who take part in restorative programs are more likely to reintegrate successfully into society, leading to lower crime rates and stronger communities (Wilson et al., 2017). Also, a longitudinal study by the Urban Institute found that youth given access to counseling, education, and employment resources after incarceration were 60% less likely to reoffend within three years (Laub & Sampson, 2019). These findings underscore the necessity of implementing comprehensive support systems that tackle the underlying reasons of criminal behavior while equipping individuals with the requisite tools for success.

Personal Insight

Throughout my years of working in the law enforcement profession, I have seen the devastating consequences of a system that focuses on punishment over restoration. Many of the young people I have met throughout the years were not afforded the opportunity to genuinely recover from their past or to imagine a different future. But in those rare moments when they were met with true understanding, guidance, and genuine opportunities, I saw transformations that defied statistical expectations. I have seen young men, previously considered lost, transform into entrepreneurs, mentors, and leaders—due to someone's faith in their potential for restoration.

Restoration does not include obliterating the past; rather, it involves reshaping the future. A culture of excellence is established by choosing to encourage rather than criticize, recognizing potential instead of failure, and giving individuals the resources to reclaim their lives. True excellence is measured by our capacity to rekindle hope where it was once believed lost.

Enrich:
Creating Opportunities for Growth and Success

Enrichment is the catalyst for growth, transformation, and sustained success. It nurtures individuals and organizations, helping them to reach their full potential by promoting an environment where individuals feel inspired, empowered, and prepared to thrive. When companies invest in comprehensive development—encompassing education, leadership, creativity, and personal growth—they foster a legacy of success and fulfillment.

Enrichment goes beyond academics or vocational training; it includes moments that ignite passion, build resilience, and promote self-discovery. Engaging in arts, athletics, entrepreneurship, or community service offers individuals significant experiences that enable them to envision a future filled with purpose and potential. Engagement in enriching activities develops critical thinking, leadership skills, and a sense of belonging, all vital for sustained success.

Enrichment is the practice of promoting lifelong learning, growth, and self-improvement in ways that go beyond traditional education. It is about providing opportunity for individuals to broaden their perspectives, discover their passions, and build the skills required to thrive in a quickly changing world. Organizations and communities that value enrichment create an environment in which people feel encouraged and challenged to achieve their full potential. This enrichment culture helps more than just individuals; it also enhances families, companies, and communities by encouraging innovation, resilience, and a commitment to greatness.

Mentorship and guidance are among the most effective strategies to foster enrichment. When people have access to mentors who can provide insight, support, and practical wisdom, they acquire a road map to success that would otherwise be difficult to follow. Mentorship programs connect young people with experts, business owners, and educators who can lead them through their personal and professional development. These partnerships boost confidence, broaden perspectives, and introduce mentees to opportunities they may not have explored before.

Leadership development is another essential part of enrichment. Encouraging people to take up leadership roles, whether in schools, companies, or community organizations, fosters important skills like communication, problem-solving, and teamwork. Individuals who complete leadership training programs are more equipped to make informed decisions, inspire others, and effectively manage obstacles. Organizations that nurture leadership skills in young people make sure the next generation is ready to take on responsibilities and achieve meaningful change.

Enrichment is closely tied to the arts and creative expression. Creativity is more than just artistic aptitude; it is about thinking critically, solving issues differently, and presenting ideas confidently. Individuals can express themselves and improve personally through programs that promote music, theater, visual arts, and creative writing. These activities encourage people to try new things, develop emotional intelligence, and find a sense of purpose. The arts also encourage cultural understanding, letting people respect different backgrounds and perspectives.

Athletics and physical activity are also important for personal development and enrichment. Sports promote discipline, collaboration, and perseverance—qualities required for success in any industry. Aside from the physical benefits, athletics teach qualities like commitment, goal-setting, and resilience. Sports programs that emphasize character development teach people how to deal with failures, work together, and push themselves beyond their apparent limits. These teachings apply directly to academics, career, and personal success.

Another effective way to enrich oneself is through entrepreneurship. Individuals learn the principles of business ownership, financial literacy, and strategic thinking, which prepares them for self-sufficiency and success. Entrepreneurial initiatives that foster creativity and invention enable people to take control of their financial future, improve their problem-solving skills, and contribute to economic progress. Early exposure to entrepreneurship helps young individuals gain confidence in their capacity to originate ideas, take calculated risks, and make their dreams a reality.

Enrichment also includes community involvement and volunteerism. Service initiatives foster a strong sense of duty, empathy, and social awareness. Volunteering lets people observe personally the influence of their efforts, which fosters a sense of purpose and connection to the larger community. Organizations that promote service-based learning foster cultures in which people understand the value of giving back and making a positive difference.

Enrichment includes lifelong learning and constant self-improvement. In today's fast-paced environment, people must be adaptive and eager to learn new skills throughout their life. Organizations that encourage continuous professional development make sure staff remain competitive in their areas while also cultivating a culture of inquiry and progress. Giving people access to workshops, training sessions, and higher education options lets them improve their abilities, stay ahead of industry trends, and pursue new interests.

An enriching atmosphere focuses on personal well-being and overall growth. Mental and emotional health impact an individual's ability to succeed, and organizations that invest in wellness initiatives foster more productive and engaged communities. Programs that teach stress management, mindfulness, and work-life balance help people develop resilience and motivation. When people feel intellectually and emotionally supported, they are more inclined to explore chances for growth and make constructive contributions to their communities.

The digital age has also created new chances for enrichment, such as online study, virtual mentorship, and worldwide networking. Digital platforms provide access to a lot of materials that let individuals broaden their knowledge, connect with experts in other industries, and develop skills that relate to their aspirations. Technology, whether as online courses, podcasts, webinars, or virtual conferences, has made enrichment more accessible than ever.

Lastly, enrichment is about unleashing potential and fostering a culture in which people feel encouraged to dream big and take meaningful actions toward their goals. It is about more than just obtaining knowledge; it is about instilling curiosity, creativity, and a lifetime dedication to personal growth. Organizations and communities that engage in enrichment develop individuals who are prepared for success and capable of making a permanent impact on the world.

When enrichment is a fundamental value, people thrive in situations that promote curiosity, skill development, and pursuing excellence. It guarantees that people have access to the tools, resources, and support they need to realize their amazing potential. A society that values enrichment cultivates leaders, innovators, and changemakers who propel development and inspire future generations. Organizations that commit to continual learning, personal growth, and meaningful experiences leave a legacy of greatness that lasts well beyond the present, paving the way for a future of limitless prospects and sustained prosperity.

Example: Youth Leadership and Entrepreneurship Initiative

A city collaborated with local businesses and nonprofit organizations to establish a youth leadership and entrepreneurship project. The curriculum offered practical instruction in financial literacy, business development, and leadership abilities. A participant, who was initially underperforming academically and directionless, uncovered a passion for business through the program. With guidance and resources, she successfully established a small business, then turning it into a flourishing venture that now employs other young individuals in her community. Her transition from uncertainty to business underscores the transformative potential of enrichment in changing lives.

Supporting Data

According to the National Endowment for the Arts (2012), "students with a low socioeconomic status (SES) that have a history of involvement in the arts have better long-term academic, occupational, and social outcomes than their peers" (p. 17). Also, the U.S. Chamber of Commerce Foundation (2015) reports that "half of employers are unable to fill vacant positions and only 11% of employers feel newly credentialed graduates are ready for work," underscoring the importance of entrepreneurial programs in enhancing youth employment rates and promoting long-term financial stability (p. 5). These findings show the need for integrating entrepreneurship and the arts into career readiness and leadership capacity to improve the outcomes for young people.

Personal Insight

Throughout my career, I have seen the significant influence of enrichment programs on youth. Most of the youngsters I found in law enforcement had not been afforded opportunities to pursue their abilities or passions. Absent proper engagement, people often resorted to destructive alternatives. Seeing the impact of mentorship, education, and creative channels on their life reinforced my conviction that investing in enrichment is not merely useful —it is imperative.

Enrichment is fundamental to a flourishing community. By offering individuals the opportunity to realize their potential, we cultivate a culture where brilliance is the norm rather than the exception. A culture of excellence prospers when individuals are surviving and genuinely thriving.

Sustaining a Culture of Excellence: Long-Term Commitment to Change

A culture of excellence is not a short-term initiative; it is a sustained commitment that requires ongoing cultivation and reinforcement. Establishing a strong foundation via the CULTURE framework is the initial step; however, the true challenge is in maintaining that culture. Organizations, educational institutions, and communities must be deliberate in their efforts to maintain and advance their commitment to excellence.

Overcoming Challenges

All initiatives, despite their intentions, will face challenges. Resistance to change, constantly shifting priorities, and leadership changes can jeopardize the sustainability of a culture of excellence. To address these difficulties, organizations must integrate the principles of CULTURE into their values and operational strategies. This requires:

- Clear and Consistent Communication: Leaders must consistently repeat the vision and principles of excellence, making sure each member of the organization comprehends their responsibility in maintaining it.

- Commitment at All Levels: A culture of excellence cannot be exclusively driven by leadership; it must be adopted by everybody, from executives to frontline staff and community stakeholders.

- Proactive Problem-Solving: Anticipating issues and mitigating them before escalation can prevent setbacks in cultural transformation.

The Role of Leadership in Maintaining Excellence

Leaders help to maintain a culture of excellence. Their actions, decisions, and engagement significantly affect an organization's adherence to its values. Competent leaders:

- Model the Behavior They Expect: Leaders who personify the principles of CULTURE establish the benchmark for others to emulate.

- Empower and Develop Others: Committing to professional growth and mentorship makes sure future leaders are equipped to maintain a culture of excellence.

- Hold Themselves and Others Accountable: Regular evaluations and feedback systems help set high standards and reinforce a culture of continual improvement.

Measuring Impact

To maintain excellence, companies must track progress and evaluate the effectiveness of their actions. This can be done through:

- Key Performance Indicators (KPIs): Metrics such as staff engagement, retention rates, and youth program success rates can offer insights into cultural sustainability.

- Surveys and Feedback Mechanisms: Consistent input from employees, students, or community members guarantees that the culture remains attuned to their needs.

- Case Studies and Success Stories: Documenting and distributing stories of transformation reinforces the importance of maintaining a culture of excellence.

Community and Stakeholders Engagement

A culture of excellence transcends the organization, it thrives through engagement with stakeholders such as families, businesses, policymakers, and local institutions. Interacting with the larger community guarantees that the influence is widespread and able to be maintained. Strategies for engagement include:

- Collaboration with Local Organizations: Partnering with organizations, corporations, and civic entities can provide more resources and assistance.

- Continuous Training and Workshops: Ongoing education guarantees that all individuals stay aligned with the standards of excellence.

- Public Acknowledgment and Celebrations: Recognizing accomplishments and milestones keeps motivation high and emphasizes the significance of the cultural transformation.

Adapting to Changing Needs

Excellence requires adaptability. As societal demands change, organizations must remain adaptable in adjusting their methods while upholding their beliefs. This means:

- Tracking Emerging Trends: Staying abreast of research and best practices guarantees organizational effectiveness.

- Innovating While Upholding Core Values: New methods and technologies can augment cultural initiatives without compromising foundational principles.

- Fostering a Growth Mindset: A dedication to perpetual learning and improvement keeps the culture dynamic and relevant.

Final Thoughts

A culture of excellence is a continuous endeavor, not a final destination. It requires dedication, adaptation, and unwavering adherence to the core principles of CULTURE. By integrating these principles into all facets of a business and consistently reinforcing them, leaders can guarantee that their influence continues for future generations. Excellence is not a singular accomplishment; it is a lifestyle, nurtured and maintained through deliberate actions and a steadfast commitment to being a difference-maker and change agent in society.

Conclusion:
Building a Future Where Everyone Thrives

Aculture of excellence requires both vision and unwavering dedication. It is a commitment to make deliberate decisions that elevate individuals, empower communities, and redefine success. While challenges are unavoidable, pursuing greatness is not about achieving perfection—it is about constantly pushing to be better, do more, and help others otherwise left behind. The CULTURE framework serves as a blueprint for this transformation, but its success ultimately depends on the collective efforts of leaders, educators, business owners, parents, and community members.

Excellence does not occur in isolation. It thrives when organizations and individuals collaborate on a common goal to inspire, educate, and empower. A community that cares will discover ways to provide mentorship and assistance, making sure no one is left to face life's challenges alone. Understanding serves as a bridge between intentions and meaningful action, showing past surface-level obstacles and address the underlying causes of systemic crises. We develop trust and collaboration by listening to others. Teaching is a long-term investment that gives students the skills and information they need to succeed. Properly using resources makes sure opportunities are available to everybody, not just those with inherent advantages. Restoring dignity and confidence offers second opportunities, which can result in astonishing transformations. Finally, enrichment maintains momentum by keeping people interested, motivated, and inspired to achieve their full potential.

The responsibility to create this culture does not rest exclusively on organizations, government programs, or school systems. It is a shared responsibility that applies to everyone with the power to influence others. Each of us impacts the world, whether at home, work, or in the broader community. The responsibility to create this culture does not rest exclusively on organizations, government programs, or school systems. A kind word, a listening ear, or an opportunity extended at the right moment can change the course of a person's life.

Creating a culture of excellence means raising the standard for leadership. Leaders must hold themselves accountable to the same principles they expect from others. Leadership is not about authority alone—it is about service, integrity, and the ability to inspire people toward a common goal. The most effective leaders understand that their most important legacy is not the titles they hold or the accolades they receive, but the lives they positively influence. Whether leading a family, a corporation, a school, or a nonprofit, individuals who embody the principles of CULTURE serve as catalysts for progress.

A commitment to excellence means a commitment to ongoing development. It requires a willingness to adapt, learn, and evolve in response to new opportunities and challenges. The world is constantly changing, and our approaches to leadership, education, and community development must evolve alongside it. Those that value lifelong learning and seek innovative solutions will be in the best position to drive meaningful change. By remaining open to new ideas, fostering collaboration across different sectors, and encouraging diverse perspectives, we create a culture that is dynamic and forward-thinking.

At the heart of this movement is the belief that everyone has untapped potential waiting to be discovered. Some may require only a gentle nudge in the correct direction, but others may require significant assistance to overcome deeply rooted barriers. Despite the starting point, the end goal is the same: to inspire people to rise above limitations, embrace their abilities, and contribute to society. When we invest in people, we do not just change individual lives—we strengthen entire communities, making sure future generations inherit a world defined by opportunity rather than limitation.

Our actions today shape the legacy we will leave behind. Will we choose to be passive observers of the challenges facing our society, or will we take decisive steps to create real and lasting change? Will we allow cycles of crime, poverty, and despair to continue, or will we intervene with mentorship, education, and leadership to transforms lives? The answers to these questions will define the future, not only for the people we serve, but for generations to come.

It is easy to become discouraged in the face of adversity, but history has shown that resilience, determination, and a clear sense of purpose can overcome even the most formidable challenges. Pursuing excellence is not always an easy route, but it is always rewarding. Each step forward, no matter how small, brings us closer to a society where every individual has the opportunity to succeed.

This is more than a call to action; it is an invitation to be part of something greater than ourselves. Whether you are a parent, a business owner, an educator, a mentor, or simply someone who believes in the power of positive change, your role in shaping the future is invaluable. Together, we can build a world where excellence is not the exception but the expectation—a world where every child, every employee, and every leader have the tools they need to thrive.

Let us take the responsibility seriously. Let us seize the opportunity to lead, guide, and transform. Proverbs 22:6 states, "Train up a child in the way he should go, and when he is old, he will not depart from it." This should be our guiding philosophy as we strive to leave a legacy of greatness for future generations.

References

American Psychological Association. (2002). *Developing adolescents: A reference for professionals*. APA.

https://www.apa.org/topics/teens/developing-adolescents-professionals-reference

Brown, B. (2018). *Dare to lead: Brave work. Tough conversations. Whole hearts.* Random House.

Cornell Chronicle. (2021, June 16). Managers who listen attract top talent. *Cornell Chronicle.*

https://www.ilr.cornell.edu/news/research/managers-who-listen-attract-top-talent

Harrison, M., & Gorman, J. (2017). The impact of trauma-informed care and active listening in youth rehabilitation. *Journal of Juvenile Justice and Rehabilitation, 12*(3), 105-121.

Kurtz, D. (2015). Structured recreation programming can help reduce juvenile crime. *Parks & Recreation Magazine.*

Laub, J. H., & Sampson, R. J. (2019). *Shared beginnings, divergent lives: Delinquent boys to age 70.* Harvard University Press.

Learning Policy Institute. (n.d.). *Improving student outcomes through restorative practices.*

https://learningpolicyinstitute.org/product/restorative-practices-factsheet

Liu, A. M., & Parilla, J. (2022). *Federal investments in sector-based training can boost workers' upward mobility.* Brookings Institution.

https://www.brookings.edu/articles/federal-investments-in-sector-based-training-can-boost-workers-upward-mobility/

Mackinac Center for Public Policy. (2023). *Research finds prison education programs reduce recidivism.*

https://www.mackinac.org/pressroom/2023/research-finds-prison-education-programs-reduce-recidivism

MENTOR: The National Mentoring Partnership. (2014). *The mentoring effect: Young people's perspectives on the outcomes and availability of mentoring.* MENTOR.

https://www.mentoring.org/wp-content/uploads/2019/11/The-Mentoring-Effect_Full-Report.pdf

National Dropout Prevention Center: National Dropout Prevention Center. (n.d.). *Economic impacts of dropouts.* NDPC.

https://dropoutprevention.org/resources/statistics/quick-facts/economic-impacts-of-dropouts

National Endowment for the Arts. (2012). *The arts and achievement in at-risk youth: Findings from four longitudinal studies.* https://www.arts.gov

National Youth Employment Coalition. (2020). *Jobs and training for youth with justice involvement: How WIOA funding can help.*

https://nyec.org/2020/12/jobs-and-training-for-youth-with-justice-involvement-how-wioa-funding-can-help/

Steinberg, L. (2014). *Age of opportunity: Lessons from the new science of adolescence.* Houghton Mifflin Harcourt.

U.S. Chamber of Commerce Foundation. (2015). *Talent orchestrators: Scaling youth employment through business-facing intermediaries.*

https://www.uschamberfoundation.org/education/talent-orchestrators-scaling-youth-employment-through-business-facing-intermediaries

U.S. Department of Labor: U.S. Department of Labor. (2019). *Reentry employment opportunities: Supporting reentry employment.* DOL.

https://www.dol.gov/sites/dolgov/files/ETA/publications/ETAOP2019-11%20REO%20Supporting%20Reentry%20Employment%20RB090319.pdf

Walton, G. M., Okonofua, J. A., Cunningham, K. R., Hurst, D., Pinedo, A., Weitz, E., Ospina, J. P., Tate, H., & Eberhardt, J. L. (2021). Lifting the bar: A relationship-orienting intervention reduces recidivism among children reentering school from juvenile detention. *Psychological Science*, 32(8), 1243–1255. https://doi.org/10.1177/09567976211013801

Wilson, D. B., Olaghere, A., & Kimbrell, C. S. (2017). Effectiveness of restorative justice principles in juvenile justice: A meta-analysis. *National Institute of Justice.*

Zavala, M. (2023, October 15). *Do after-school programs reduce delinquency?* Afterschool.org.

https://afterschool.org/do-after-school-programs-reduce-delinquency/

Zehr, H. (2015). *The little book of restorative justice.* Good Books.

James Thomas, ED.D.